T0243518

THE PRIDE LIST

EDITED BY SANDIP ROY AND BISHAN SAMADDAR

The Pride List presents works of queer literature to the world.
An eclectic collection of books of queer stories, poems,
plays, biographies, histories, thoughts, ideas, experiences
and explorations, the Pride List does not focus on any specific
region, nor on any specific genre, but celebrates the great diversity
of LGBTQ+ lives across countries, languages, centuries and
identities, with the conviction that queer pride comes from its
unabashed expression.

Valentijn Hoogenkamp

ANTIBOY

Translated from the Dutch by
MICHELE HUTCHISON

LONDON NEW YORK CALCUTTA

N ederlands
letterenfonds
dutch foundation
for literature

The publisher gratefully acknowledges the
support of the Dutch Foundation for Literature

Seagull Books, 2024

First published in Dutch as *Antiboy*

Antiboy © 2022 Valentijn Hoogenkamp.
Originally published by De Bezige Bij, Amsterdam

First published in English translation by Seagull Books, 2024

English translation © Michele Hutchison, 2024

The sentence 'What a funny place to rupture' on page 6 is quoted
from Frank O'Hara's poem 'Mayakovsky' from the volume
Meditations in an Emergency (1957).

The quotation on pages 58–59 is a transcript from an exchange between
contestants Tiffany Pollard and Gemma Collins in an episode of the UK
television show *Celebrity Big Brother*, Series 17 (2016), broadcast on
Channel 5. Included here with kind permission.

The unusual layout on of page 8 is intentional.

ISBN   978 1 8030 9 422 9

British Library Cataloguing-in-Publication Data
A catalogue record for this book is available from the British Library

Typeset by Seagull Books, Calcutta, India
Printed and bound in the USA by Integrated Books International

ANTIBOY

I COME FROM a long line of liars. When she moved to the Netherlands from Suriname's capital Paramaribo in 1933, my great-grandmother lied when she said she wasn't Jewish. My grandmother lied to the man she was married to on the island of Aruba. She said she'd come back as she ran away to the Netherlands with her baby. She left behind her other child, a four-year-old girl who would one day grow up to be my mother. My father lied the time I asked him whether he and my mother loved each other and he said they didn't, they were more like friends, but still, it's impossible for me to see his life as anything other than one big attempt to win my mother's affections. My sister Toni lied when she said that I was the only child in our family with emotions and that she didn't have any.

I feel their proximity when I wake up from the operation, but it's just Mort and Charlotte sitting next to my bed, and my mum. But no, she isn't here, if I ever see her again I'll beat her to death with a big diamond. The first time I came round from the anaesthetic, in the recovery room, there was a woman on the other side of the curtain screaming that they'd scraped her baby out of her, and my chest was numb. My mouth hung open, dribble collected in my cheek. Tubes ran right and left from my armpits to two plastic bottles filled with red liquid. I flapped my arms cautiously but barely lifted off the ground.

'I'm awake,' I mumbled. My throat was sore from the tube. I had been on a ventilator. When was that again? This morning.

'They stole my baby,' the woman cried.

'Hush now,' a professional voice reassured her.

I am [reborn] awake. Someone promises to get me an ice lolly, but the screaming woman has put me off. Her panic seeps through the curtain and the blood I can see doesn't belong in a bottle but inside me. I just want to get out of here. My sweet boyfriend Mort is slumped in a chair; when I open my eyes he smiles. He is unbelievably good at smiling. While I was asleep, Charlotte painted me a get-well card with a portable watercolour set. She says she almost became a nurse rather than an artist and helps me drink from a plastic beaker. I try to thank them but blow spit bubbles instead.

Once I'm given a new injection of morphine, I'm off like a rocket.

'When the revolution breaks out, I think we should use violence,' I say. 'Mort is a pacifist but that's no use, it means others will have to get their hands dirty for him.'

'Violence only begets violence. Murdering other people is ridiculous,' Mort says and Charlotte shakes her head. She can't believe we're talking about this. Just as Mort gets up to go make a phone call in the hall, the doctor arrives for the first check.

The doctor asks whether I'm ready to see my wounds. I feel Charlotte's soft hands on my back as I sit upright, her fingers opening the compression vest, assisted by the doctor. The pattern of the zip is engraved deeply into my skin, between two bloodied strips of encrusted gauze where my breasts used to be.

What a funny place to rupture.

After the doctor has gone, I ask Charlotte to hand me the purple hortensia which is in a vase by my bed. A friend brought it for me, I want to hold it to my flat chest in both hands. I float downstream on waves of morphine, a corpse on its way to a seaman's grave.

I feel like crying when visiting hours end, but Mort has to appear on a talk show and Charlotte is going to a wedding in Almere. Convinced I've lost them forever, I lie sweating under a fleece blanket.

My sister advised me to stay in hospital as long as possible, they have really good drugs and they won't send me home until I can pee on my own. I ring for someone to help me to the toilet. Nurse Judith is standing by when I push myself up and swing my legs over the edge of the bed, but she is too late to catch me when I fall against a chair. The bottles containing wound discharge shoot loose and spill red across the linoleum floor. A white beeping fills my mind and flashes behind my eyes.

'There's still a bit over there,' I whisper to Judith, who is busying herself with a cloth. I don't want to sleep surrounded by blood.

When I come to in the dark, a Flemish night nurse is standing at my bedside. He is supposed to check how much fluid is still coming from the wounds and he doesn't understand why one of the bottles is empty and there are no stickers on it. I'm not sure I'm talking sense about the fall, but he has already understood.

'That's our Judith,' the night nurse sighs as he labels my bottles.

I try to make the darkness my ally. On the bed next to mine, a phone screen glows and, after hesitating, I also grab my phone and untangle my earphones. In the corridor, a man is wandering around, crying; he has Alzheimer's and doesn't understand that he's not allowed to eat or drink. The nurses let him sit with them in their illuminated office. The hard plastic pods keep falling from my ears. With swollen fingers, I try to type the name of the talk show Mort is appearing on, but the words   all wobbly and who has sent me a heart? Nearly manage to send   a heart back, but my fingers are   too   no   Mort has sent a message no

a video of host Humberto Tan, filmed on Mort's phone, Humberto telling me to get well soon.

I can see from Humberto's eyes that he likes Mort and is happy to do this for him, so the talk show must have gone well. The video message is followed by silence and black. The darkness is a tunnel in which I call out for my mother, but she rides away on her blue motor-bike. Just before she died, she begged for her own mother, and grandma was brought to her in her wheelchair.

'Mum,' my mother sobbed, and Grandma wept too and said, 'I was supposed to go first.'

'Why are you in a wheelchair?' my mum asked in amazement, undoing the years.

Motionless, I lie in my hospital bed through the long night, missing her and the friends I no longer talk to. The fleece blanket slides down to my ankles. They need to pump up the morphine, please, please. My mum is somewhere in the dark, and when I walk over to her the water comes up to my waist.

The water sucks at my shirt, which is swirling around me. Dancing circles, the smell of a stagnant ditch in the sun and flies swarm just above. My boots have filled up and sink into the goo. I pinch my nose and duck down. Underwater it is quiet, no beeps from the drip. A green hum presses against my eardrums. Lips pursed, eyelids squeezed shut. I am seven and something is wrong with my face. Given that I will never have different bones and cannot pull off my skin, I decide to drown myself in the ditch at the end of the schoolyard. Bubbles escape from my nose and nestle in my eyebrows.

Open your mouth.

No.

Gasping for breath, I launch myself and sink deeper into the muddy bottom, waving my arms wildly, a whistling in my ears. I inhale, water gushes in, gross and brackish, but the surface breaks. Sand crunches between my teeth, I retch brown water over my shirt.

I hate dying. It fucking hurts. I hate my parents for being at work miles away and my classmates who don't want to play with me. I hate my arms and legs and chin without a dimple. It's shallow here and the water still comes up to my nipples. The ditch gleams greasily in the sun. I slap the grease patches with both hands, harder and harder.

A man gets out of his car in front of the Showboat, a floating swingers' club moored further up, he doesn't even look my way. Cars race past on the road by the ditch, beyond them the meadows begin and then the sky. The wind sweeps low over the water and I shiver in my wet T-shirt. I don't think I understood before that you can just fall into a crack like this. Not because people don't love you but because no one knows where you are.

Slosh slosh slosh go my socks on the paving stones. My boots left behind in the goo. They were old-lady boots, my mother has no taste. I am a coward, I think, such a big coward. The schoolyard pulsates. Without making eye contact, I walk among the playing children, past the patter of a skipping rope, and with tearful eyes it dawns on me that I could have just gone to the back of the skipping queue and waited my turn.

They always stare like that. On school trips, they can all see me standing in the aisle of the bus clutching my backpack. They know why I get to sit in the front next to the teacher even though I never get carsick. No one to walk hand in hand to the gym with, to go around the classes with on my birthday.

'Hey, you're all wet,' Jacqueline says. She lowers the skipping rope and comes over to me with the girls. One volunteers to go and fetch the teacher and when I lie, saying I slipped near the ditch, they nod. My hair clings to my cheeks in muddy strands, long hair just like theirs. Their shoulders in cotton shirts, a

11

hand held out to pat my back as though I were choking. I can do this. I have the same arms and legs as them, I am approximately the same size. I can be one of them.

'TRY ADDING A BELT,' Mum said when she saw me drowning in the dress with the rose pattern.

A skinny leather belt that gave me a waist. Her shoes were too big, so I wore white sports socks and insoles, but my feet kept slipping. I'd roll up the sleeves of sweaters she passed on to me, but she stubbornly kept insisting that we were the same size.

A year before the breast operation, I spread every item of clothing I own on the floor, all the way to the dining-room table's curled wooden legs. The table comes from the house I grew up in, and above it my parents' lamp casts golden circles of light on the table-top; their old curtains hang at the windows. Only the sofa is mine, given to me by two people who used to let their dogs sleep on it. So many of Mum's dresses, Mum's earrings, Mum's fake pearls.

The woman she wanted me to become delineates herself on the floor, lying there in the empty casing of her clothes, among her worn furniture, taking over my house. Sitting cross-legged, I stuff the dresses into bin bags. Exuberant floral patterns, dots, stripes, everything disappears. I lean against the sofa, which I regularly shift from one corner of the room to the other. Mort gets nervous about that. It's not a big room, the sofa never disappears. Tired, I rub my hair. Put it up, Mum always said. She thought loose hair was scruffy and cheap, like sticky lipstick. Reaching behind my head, I pull the clip loose, the strands fall over my shoulders and breasts.

'But you're not getting rid of that dress with the roses, are you? It used to be your favourite,' her hopeful voice coos. I put it on over my tracksuit, my hands in my sides to create a waist. The girl in the mirror does the same, her eyes are dull.

My favourite dress, my safety net, the one that came with me to every country I went to. It worked everywhere. *You really are one of those 1960s girls*, said a man in his sixties in a party tent on a lawn. The dress that meant I didn't have to talk but be talked to, leaned against so I couldn't get away. It matched my red hair. Have I ever had a normal conversation in that dress? I shake my head, my reflection doesn't join in, she looks down and smooths her skirt.

'You can still wear clumpy shoes with it,' she mutters. 'It's just a piece of fabric. It doesn't matter, it's not real.'

Is this the face that launched a thousand ships? my English teacher quoted as the sixteen-year-old me breezed into his class with a frown. A round face framed by wavy hair and a dress like a robe to be worn on the foredeck of a warship.

'Thank you,' I say to the red-and-white dress before fastening the bin bag. The cotton roses bow their heads.

My appetite for destruction is making me sea-sick, so I go up to the attic to write. My desk is at a window covered in moss. There's a mess behind my chair, an unsteady pile of photo albums, a box of toys and ballpoint pens, unread books that I slide off the shelf when I'm looking for something. But I sit with my back to the mess, I only look at the window, the green light it casts onto my notebooks.

For days I've been walking around with a speech in my head that an actor once gave when collecting an award. He claimed that the acting profession involves being the Other. It sounds good but *acting* isn't the same as *being*. You can't stop *being* at the end of the day. As I try to lay my finger on it, I start to write— today a scene about a boy and a girl trying on each other's clothes. To the boy it's a game, he's still a bodybuilder even when he's wearing a top with spaghetti straps. He flexes his muscles making the pink vest bulge. The girl drowns in his hoody and his trousers. She looks at him in the mirror, at herself and then bursts into tears. For her it's not a game.

I put down my pen. The green attic window is open, outside pigeons coo in the ivy-covered tree. I know whose muscles they are, those of my second boyfriend, and I know whose hoody it is, it belongs to the boy I lost my virginity to, I even know whose pink spaghetti top it is, it's the girl who kissed me in the club and then fell into a deep sleep, beside me on the airbed, no longer interested when nobody was looking at us. I know whose broken heart it is when he looks in the mirror and sees a little girl, when I squint I see a teenage boy, but never a man with muscles that could be accentuated by a tiny pink top.

Downstairs I go. I gaze in confusion at the crime scene of washed-up bin bags in the sitting room. Not full of limbs but dresses that are too big, and sneakers. All of the bags need opening and emptying out onto the floor before I find the rose-print dress again. This time I take off all my clothes before I put it on. I apply lipstick and comb my hair into place.

I know how to create a cowboy. My leather boots, a certain no-one-can-touch-me swagger as I head to the supermarket, flamboyantly swing open the doors to the refrigerated sections and run my hands along the cold packets of spinach. I'm even better at imitating a girl. She thinks it's glamorous to stride across the zebra crossing in high heels and flares. People often start telling her their life story for no reason. She fantasizes about taking a bullet for someone she loves. The most important thing about this girl is that she exists in between me and other people. They look at her and I look at her.

The girl brought me closer to other girls. Surrounded by girlfriends, lying on a bed together just before going out. If they knew about me, I wouldn't be able to lie here or get so close to them as they get changed. They all kissed me and for me it wasn't a joke. We were fifteen, put on make-up, sent text messages on our Nokias. Gossip floated through the room like the scent of roses. Tatjana had a cigarette burn on her lower back. Had she gone skinny dipping with the boys we met last night? She denied it, and Maud insisted on proof, she wanted to see the burn hole in the top Tatjana had been wearing. She said she didn't know where the top was and that Maud was a sad case, she'd spent the night on the phone to her boyfriend, and that wasn't very sociable, the rest of us thought, was it? I agreed with everyone else. Pauline reached over my face to put down her mobile and I instinctively bit into her flesh like a puppy. She looked at me with her soft arm still in my mouth. No one had noticed because everyone was talking.

That girl also brought me closer to the boys who complained to me that the other girls were bitchy and ignored them. The girls didn't notice me either, not really, though I understood better than the boys that you didn't have a God-given right to anything and I never said, 'I ought to behave like a bastard really.'

I look in the mirror at my lipsticked lips and summer dress, waves of hair falling past my ears. Anti, where are you? Not with my mum, I never wanted to see her when she was ill. I let train after train depart as I roamed around the station, ignoring the vibrations from my phone, and giving myself crying eyes at the chemists with plum eyeliner. Two days before she died, I was working at home, immersed in a laptop full of emails I urgently had to answer, yes urgently. She'd excused me from having to stay at her house, saying that *if I wasn't there for myself, I couldn't be there for her*. But I'd promised both of us that I'd be there that day. I saw too late that it was already four o'clock. Cycling as fast as I could to the station, I didn't realize I'd forgotten my travelcard until I reached the barriers. I didn't deliberately miss the train, but how could she know the difference after I'd invented so many disruptions to the rail services.

It didn't really matter that I wouldn't come that day after all, she said, because by the time I'd cycled home and back with the travelcard, it would be an hour later and she'd probably already be asleep. Maybe I shouldn't listen to my voicemail messages. The next day they attached an analgesic drip which slowly put her to sleep. I'd missed her last day of mental clarity. After her funeral, I listened to my voicemail.

She repeated my name in a tiny voice, asking time after time, 'Where are you, Anti?'

I wish I could forget that. Put it in the bin bags along with her dresses, along with that invented girl who made her so proud, or in any case, didn't worry her. I call Slimane on impulse, he never picks up anyway, and almost hang up when I hear his voice.

'Yeah?'

And I ask, 'Slimane, how did you know you were trans?'

'SLIMANE IS A GHOST,' I wrote in my diary. When I was nineteen, I moved into an apartment in Amsterdam with a bedroom and a living room. The girl I rented my room from slept in the living room. There was no door. When I was in the kitchen, I could hear her when she had sex, sounds that became familiar and never stopped at the sound of my footsteps or the ping of the microwave. Muted chats and laughter and my name whispered from time to time.

As a child I'd already made several attempts to keep a diary, the same way I liked staring melancholically into rivers or lakes or the sea. They sold diaries with golden locks in the supermarket, I'd laid several out ready on my desk. As soon as I'd written anything, my mum would put the diary in the loo so that guests had something to read. You could open the locks with your thumbs, so I left most of the pages empty, or I lied that I was in love with a boy called Jonas but he'd fallen for my best friend, a ménage à trois I'd taken from a television show. I didn't have a best friend.

It was only at the kitchen table in my new home, with my flatmate's moans and occasional shrieks in the background, that I began to write without the risk of anyone reading it. It was about Slimane, who had just disappeared from my life at the time. She had stopped answering her phone and after forty-nine days I wrote in my diary: *It's been forty-nine days since I last spoke to you. Yesterday and the day before that I didn't think about you.*

Her pubic hair rubbed my cheeks as I did my best under her feather duvet. Her belly stayed cool no matter how many kisses I planted on it, but that was nice for my forehead because it was suffocatingly hot under the duvet. We both had vaginas, which was why I thought this would be simple, but I felt like I was fourteen again, the first time I'd tried to pleasure a boy and almost choked on the rubbery lube of his banana-flavoured condom. It didn't taste like real bananas but the sweets. After all the hairy men I'd been to bed with, I found her body really smooth. I was amazed that my arm almost fit entirely around her waist. She guided me with her thighs and hands, grabbed the back of my head and pushed me downwards. I touched her cautiously, dipped fingertips into her, maybe too gently, I was so keen to do it well the first time, I wished it was over already.

She'd started it a few weeks earlier, she'd kissed me on a train we'd taken together. She just grabbed my chin roughly and I froze like a rabbit watching the movements of a beautiful snake. Slimane had a shock of curls she hid her face behind. Her mouth was slightly crooked, she looked different in photos than in real life. She hated being photographed and her shuddering laugh rarely showed in her eyes. Next came weeks of squeezing and tickling each other and sneaking off together when we were with fellow students. Slimane pinning me to a wall in some corridor and blowing on my lips, writing down titles of songs I should listen to in my notebooks. 'Romeo and Juliet' by Dire Straits. 'I Want You' by Elvis Costello. 'The First Cut Is the Deepest', P. P. Arnold, and I looked for coded messages in the lyrics of all those break-up songs.

There was another girl I'd made out with, together with my first boyfriend. I was crazy about her and had wanted to make that clear with a threesome. First, my boyfriend made us some peanut-butter sandwiches so that we'd be less drunk and could make the decision more rationally. A peanut was still stuck behind a molar when I gave him a blowjob. It had been enjoyable and sweet but when I described the experience to Slimane, she said it didn't count because he'd been there.

The muscles in her thighs contracted, the salty taste got sweeter. She pressed herself hard against my mouth, my teeth, my tongue. I slowed down but she urged me on, taking my wrist and pushing my fingers deeper inside her. Clenching around my fingers like a wedding ring, now my life had begun, *Stop* she said abruptly, throwing back the covers. Slimane pulled me up to her chest and I buried my head and sticky lips in her neck. Her hair smelled of Andrélon curl cream. I took a strand in my mouth and tugged at it gently.

'I don't think you're lesbian,' she said.

I spat out her hair. 'Why not?'

She laughed and her head disappeared beneath the covers. The room was full of the heavy smell of the incense sticks that had been burning for hours. I felt her breath on my pubic hair, felt my lower body but not her tongue, my mind was churning. The boy I'd lost my virginity to had told all his classmates on the Monday; they'd surrounded me during break and asked whether he was lying. In the end, there I was boasting about his achievements while I'd done all the work. A dreamcatcher hung in front of Slimane's window, morning light fell through it, and I thought of the birds those feathers had been attached to, of that first boy who'd been so shocked by all the gossip that he'd wanted to break up on the spot. His older sister wouldn't let him, she said doing so could be traumatic for a girl right after her first time. He was already inside me for the second time when he whispered in my ear that his sister had told him we had to stay together for at least a month.

Slimane's taste stuck to my lips and cheeks. Carefully, so that she didn't notice, I reached for the half-full beaker of lukewarm, flat Coke on the nightstand and took a sip. The bump under the covers groaned. There were goosebumps on my chest but drops of sweat at the back of my knees. Slimane's tongue was too hard. I wanted to hold her as she looked at me, murmur nonsense into her neck, and as I imagined that I became softer, opened for her fingers. Now there were two of her, buried between my legs but also with her weight on top of me, she pressed me into the mattress and I could say to that girl—

'Are you still alive?' came the muffled words from under the duvet.

'Yeah, why?'

She withdrew her fingers and wiped them on my thigh, then silence.

'Do you want to go to sleep?' I asked.

After a few seconds, she crawled first to the foot of the bed, and then to the wall, where she surfaced and said she didn't like spooning. Grey twilight flooded over her shoulders which were covered in an old cotton shirt. Soon the incense sticks would burn down to the wooden holders and set the room ablaze. My arms and legs felt swollen as though I were wearing a spacesuit and stumbling slowly across the moon's surface with tears in my eyes, perfectly round droplets that would float around my helmet in slow motion and bounce back at my eyeballs. I closed my eyes briefly and muttered *thanks* as I drifted off.

Her phone alarm made a shrill sound. I shot up in bed and saw my T-shirt and belt on the floor, hastily unbuckled a couple of hours earlier. Kicked-off shoes and coins that had rolled out of the pocket of my peeled-off jeans. That person had been as pleased as punch that she'd been undressed by a girl.

'I'm staying in bed,' Slimane mumbled sleepily. Her back was turned to me, I kissed the fabric of her shirt.

'I'll be back in a bit with a bouquet of flowers.'

'Why?'

'Because you're my first,' I said barely audibly. I gathered the coins on my knees. As I did up my laces I listened to her heavy breathing. Ultimately, I would tell her what I fantasized about, or not her but someone who looked like her, a future girl I might have more in common with. But Slimane had made that girl possible. She didn't have any make-up remover, only a half-empty tube of suncream caked in dust. I removed my runny mascara with scratchy toilet paper. The thick white cream burned like hell and crept behind my eyelids, blinking didn't help, tears trickled down my cheeks.

'Do you think I'm cute?' I asked. She was asleep.

At the bedroom door, I turned and looked at the open textbooks and the slanting roof, the half-smoked joints in the ashtray and the way she lay under the covers. The echo of her voice, gentle and mocking, 'I don't think you are . . . ' But it wasn't up to her to decide who I was.

I couldn't wait to tell the boys. The boys were my colleagues at the cinema: Michael and Glenn and Kevin and Damian. From the age of fifteen, I'd been working behind the bar until the last film finished and drank beer until late with the boys, even when I had to be at school at 8.30 the next morning. They were a couple of years older, were taking their final exams or were already at uni, they had driving licences. Leaning on the bar, they asked about my sex life and it never occurred to me to lie. It was amusing to ask me what I thought of the *Playboy* posters in the projection room, they thought it hilarious when someone gave me an ashtray in the shape of a gigantic dick.

At the cinema, we had a boss who called me up at night and left long voicemail messages. I got used to being woken with a jolt, seeing his name on the lit-up phone screen and swiping it away. The boss asked whether he could buy me clothes, he'd pay with his own money and I made sure I was never alone with him in his office. He was in his fifties and sometimes slept at his desk. He snorted lines of coke from the bar, too, and kept a blacklist of employees who had tried to mess with him. The cinema was a part-time gig for us, for him it was his life. When I told my mum about the nocturnal voicemails, she said, 'If you report this, that man will be fired and never get another job. Is that seriously what you want?'

The boys thought I should put in a complaint to head office. It turned out that the boss was also fiddling the accounts. Damian took over his position as floor manager temporarily and became our new boss. At a party, he acted drunker than he was and asked whether he could show me something in the dark corridor next to the auditorium. A month previously I had dreamed that he and his girlfriend were baking me a chocolate cake together, I wasn't surprised at all when he kissed me.

They were my friends so of course I told the boys about Slimane and they couldn't get over it. When girls bought popcorn from me, they asked me what I thought of them: too tall, too fat, nice tits? They poked me in the ribs at every low-cut top. After closing, they invited me along to the new strip club in town. Kevin paid for my entrance ticket. The room was empty, there were blue and pink illuminated poles on either side of the dance floor. A stripper was doing her thing on a block. She pressed herself to the pole as though it was a teddy bear and didn't look at us.

Lukewarm white wine was ordered for me and a shot of tequila. I turned my barstool so that my back was to the bar and I had a good view of her but Glenn gave me a tap. I was supposed to turn back around and watch via the mirror behind the bar. In silence we peered through the upturned bottles at parts of her thighs, at parts of her midriff as they slid up and down. Her toes peeped out of her high-heeled sandals. The woman stepped from the block and disappeared behind the bar. There was a little stepladder there. Taking large steps, she walked between our glasses and stopped in front of Glenn's face. She sank onto her haunches, squatted over his hands which were on the bar, and rocked her buttocks just above his fingers. There was a rubber RESPECT armband dangling around her wrist. When we worked at the cinema we were all lads, but with her in our midst, I seemed to be cut off from them. The blue light exacerbated the bags under their eyes. They didn't tip when they bought the shots. I didn't want the woman to feel cheap and laid a twenty-euro note next to my wine, but her gaze kept skipping over me. There was a dark bruise on her inner thigh. The pole must be hard. I got up and walked to the block and looked at myself in the mirrored wall by the dance floor. I saw the bar behind me, my colleagues' heads tilted, staring up at the stripper. The pink triangle of her bikini glowed in the half-darkness of the empty club. Didn't the boys see that she had checked out in her mind, the tired look the dancing woman cast at her own repeated reflections? All of her nails were varnished, except for one little toe.

After a couple of tracks of low-pulsing techno, the barman put on 'Bette Davis Eyes'. I glided over to the empty dance floor to jump around in the streams of smoke issuing from the spluttering machine. Floating in a soap bubble, my mouth half open. I copied her movements in the mirror so that we were dancing together. My hands on my hips and my hair hanging over my eyes. When I saw the expressions on my colleagues' faces, I quickly returned to my barstool. The twenty-euro note lay untouched next to my glass.

'Waste of your money,' Glenn said, slipping the note into my back pocket, too fast for me to slap away his hand. The stripper towered over us.

'She can hear you,' I whispered.

'Nah,' Glenn said, 'she'll be all drugged up.'

The stripper looked at herself in the mirror with wide, sparkling eyes and chewed gum in her empty mouth. The barman gave her a glass of water and she held it in perfect balance as she climbed the steps down from the bar. Her stiletto heel landed right next to my thumb.

'Her arse wasn't great,' Kevin said even before she'd disappeared through a sliding door. He grinned at me, the same way he'd grinned on my second workday when he'd asked whether I did anal, and I'd replied that I was scared to because of a rumour about a girl from hockey who'd torn something up there and ever since she'd had to wear a nappy under her skinny jeans. It was the same grin when my friends told me about going out and getting totally wasted and getting their dicks out and secretly pissing against the DJ's booth and spattering the boots of their dancing girlfriends, or not washing their hands after taking a dump and putting their fingers in girls' mouths. It was a grin I couldn't replicate. It called for a glint in the eye and the smell of unwashed bodies and full ashtrays and the water from a hot-dog can, of horsing about on a sports pitch and handing out punches when you were called gay, and damp towels left in sports bags.

THE COFFEE PLACE where we'd arranged to meet is empty on the Tuesday morning in question. Slimane is slumped on a sofa because of chronic back pain. I'd heard on the grapevine that he was in transition and as though the news had magically summoned him, I ran into him right after that on the street. On the advice of the gender-reassignment clinic, he'd cut off his curls. In retrospect, he didn't think it was a safe move because now he looked like a Muslim boy rather than a Muslim girl. Bus drivers, lads on the street made it clear what they thought of him. He could no longer flirt secretly with their girlfriends either. Slimane laughed, he must have told this story a lot. We exchanged phone numbers so we could meet for a coffee, even though I already had his number. It was still in my phone under his female name.

'How are you, honey?' he asks as I sit down. You never stop being Slimane's honey. He gestures at the menu. A cup of tea is cooling down next to him. We never discussed the break-up. The voicemails I kept leaving until a girlfriend said I had to let it go, just let it go.

'I've had a strange day. Did you mind me calling you?'

He says he's often a walking oracle for the gay world, a *gay elder*, that's just the way it is, and we have to support each other within the community. When you haven't seen someone for a long time, you don't start by telling them that you feel like you could drift up into the sky like a balloon at any moment. I start by summarizing the past few years: writing, relationships. Slimane calmly takes me in with his brown eyes. He has gone back to college, wanting to specialize in a form of therapy in which he becomes a fragment of another person. He tries to explain it: sometimes a person wants to hold a piece of themselves in their hands and have a conversation with it. Slimane wants to be that fragment.

'Can I share something kind of intense with you?' I say.

'Go ahead.'

'I've got a gene mutation, BRCA1. My mum had it too, she died of ovarian cancer a year ago.'

'Oh sweetheart,' he says, sitting up in his seat.

'It's a genetic mutation that is only passed down from mothers to daughters. So I unconsciously thought I couldn't have it, but then I did the test and I do have it. But the doctor said it doesn't have to be a death sentence. I can have my ovaries removed and potentially my breasts too, to limit the risk of getting cancer.'

Slimane takes my hand, we entwine our fingers. A man comes in, opens his laptop at the table in front of the window, gives us a quick glance and sighs. It would have been better to have gone for a walk, shoulder to shoulder, looking at the same trees, rather than each other's faces.

38

'Have you got anyone you can talk to about this?' he asks.

'Everyone I talk to asks me that.'

I've told a lot of people already. It never really helps. I feel guilty when they try to console me, a broken slot machine swallowing coins in vain. I have a major risk of getting cancer and each year the chance of being too late with the operations increases. The doctors advised me to have children first, without them having any idea what my life's like. Everything was explained calmly as I turned into a cloud and a helpful doctor poked a hand right through me. There were blood splatters on the tiles outside the hospital, I saw them slowly fade when I used to go there twice a week.

I lost my patience after the diagnosis. I forgot the names of friends' babies, snapped that the music was too loud everywhere, food tasted grey. I accused a friend of changing her voice, she talked so slowly. I watched in amazement as my hand picked up a cup, autonomously, and I only realized I was in the shower when I saw the water running down my belly. You need a body to have sex and in those days I seemed to be living in the curve of a teardrop.

'When I got the diagnosis, I pictured my funeral and that nobody there would really know me because I'd never spoken up. And in the conversations I had at the hospital, they kept telling me what most women would do in my situation,' I say. 'I kept wanting to look over my shoulder and see if that woman was standing behind me.'

'Because you don't feel like a woman?'

'I thought femininity was something that could be learned.'

Slimane tells me there wasn't one moment of realization for him but a whole childhood of feeling alienated because he could see something that nobody else saw. At first he thought it was a psychosis. An echo of what I've been hearing for a long time inside my head: 'I'm going crazy.'

'That's part of it,' he says, 'the doubt. Gender can be so many things, it can shift, it's not something you can get right or wrong. How long have you been thinking about this?'

'Always. But before the diagnosis, I was quite happy with my body. From the outside, you couldn't see the confusion, and that felt safe. Even when I was depressed, I made sure I looked nice. It was my mind I worried about, the thoughts . . . ' I sigh. 'Today I pictured what I would look like as a man, but a man feels just slightly too far.'

'Are you non-binary?'

'You mean something in-between?'

He takes a sip of cold tea. 'Or that you don't feel at home in any category.'

Maybe I don't need to cure myself of these thoughts. A grey layer falls from me, as though I've taken off my glasses in a romcom and suddenly turned out to be pretty. The barman puts bottles of soft drink in the fridge and the man next to us hammers away at his laptop, frowning. It's all so mundane, while we are embracing something dazzling.

'You said once that I'm not lesbian,' I say.

'Really? I'm sorry.'

'And here I am, hoping you'll teach me who I am.'

I laugh, but Slimane is looking out of the window. Maybe it *is* better not to talk about the past. Or our break-up.

I don't believe there's a mysterious person inside me waiting to be discovered. At the same time, ever since the diagnosis a *no, I don't want to just survive, something wants to reveal itself* has been growing louder. Nevertheless, there is still a spark of fear that I'm making this all up, because I make up characters all day long, I describe their childhood memories, their favourite colours, first relationships, their accent, how many toilets there were in the house they grew up in and whether they had to queue to use them. I've already invented so many people that my memories are as vague as fantasies.

I feel most like myself when I bend down to pick up fallen matches and can't fit them back into the box.

'Are you going to tell people?' Slimane asks.

'Just Mort to start with,' I say. 'He's always going on about the simplicity of enlightened waters and expressing life in its true totality.'

'What?'

'Poetry, he quotes a lot of poetry. And he's my best friend after all.'

Slimane gets up to straighten his back and I get up too, taking it as a signal that we're leaving. He wraps his arms around me and smells of the same curl cream. I almost kiss his neck.

The floor is still covered with discarded clothing and torn-open bin bags. I cling to Slimane's hug, dance around with it elatedly, until I accidentally stand on a plastic necklace, sending its fake pearls in all directions. I mustn't lose the clarity that's rushing through me. Phone in hand, I let myself fall back onto the bed. Mort has gone away for a month to write. Next week I'm going to visit him because he says he's wasting away in the back of beyond where his writing residency is located. It's cold there, he's bought new tiger-print slippers. I miss his little dancing feet, but not his socks lying around. I could wait until I see him again, but I haven't felt this cheerful in a long time. First I tell Mort in my head. He's very enthusiastic, comparing me to still waters. I may not be a girl, but I can be a place in which the sky is reflected.

Reassured, I call the real Mort. We talk about his book, his slippers, the haunted basement in the house where he's staying and the spaghetti he's eating for the fourth day in a row because he cooked too much. There's no logical moment in which to casually drop my news and I almost let it sink away again. We have to be brave and not only tell our exes. So I say it, I say I might be non-binary. Silence at the other end.

'What do you think about that?'

Again he starts talking about his tiger-print slippers and his cold feet and I keep asking questions so that the conversation doesn't stall. Is it spaghetti Bolognese? Yes, with minced meat. How many pages has he written today? Seven, me too, I say: about a body-builder flexing his muscles in a pink spaghetti top and . . . The memory of the mirror fades like a dream forgotten once you get up and start your day.

'Would you please say something?' I ask.

'You know I only like women.'

'What do you mean?'

'That I *only* like women.'

'Don't you want to ask me how I feel?'

'I'm not angry with you,' he says and hangs up.

I AM A MONSTER beneath my skin my love has glasses but cannot see this which is why I picked him I sneak along the city's walls the babies cry in their cribs I make a claw in my mitten my love praises my skin so soft in the dark teeth withdrawn when I suck I am a monster I hide my face because nobody is looking in the bus next to me a creature of light with red hair freshly washed red hair I want that too the shower avoids me droplets fall next to me I am a monster hide my eyes the screeching of bald birds bald birds too big for my head beaks pecking into my eyes outside you cannot kiss me your tongue is a worm in the tram with an arm so close that I smell another monster smaller ugly with a belly but that doesn't make me more or less of a monster just a different monster I scratch open my scales under them hard skin I grow bigger every year never better never more or less monster once you are a monster it no longer matters whether you are more or less of a monster.

'. . . aesthetically undesirable,' the plastic surgeon says.

Where are you, Anti? In a windowless consulting room. The silver-haired doctor was once the winner in a reality TV show. He won both the audience prize and the jury prize for best reconstructive surgery. He explains which implants I could get if I have my breasts removed. Since the diagnosis, my breasts have been screened once a year. Strange hands almost rip them from my body and press them as flat as possible between two X-ray plates. A month later, the test results: still clean, nothing suspect yet. But the day after the results, the malignant growth could start and only be visible a year later, on the next scan. I have just told the doctor I'd rather have a flat chest.

'. . . for a young woman like you, the belly-fat option would leave a big scar and you'll want to look good in a bikini.'

Didn't I just say I don't want implants? The conversation is recorded on my mobile phone. As I play it back to understand it better, I sketch the timeline on an envelope. After four minutes, the surgeon, in his pleasantly low voice, calls a chest without breast reconstruction 'aesthetically undesirable'. After twenty minutes, I am sitting topless on his examination table and he lifts my breast with one hand and lets it fall again. As he does so, he says I have beautiful breasts and shouldn't go for a single size smaller.

As a child, the only trans women I ever saw were on Jerry Springer's talk show. They were there because their fiancés didn't know they were trans and they had come to confess. Outrage and revulsion from the fiancés and the audience. My sympathy was always with the woman being shouted at. They were still the same person, were those men blind or something? In my childish brain, all trans people were desperate to have surgery. I thought you couldn't be trans if you were scared of doctors.

'My father-in-law is a cardiologist,' I say, 'and he actually has a heart himself. But you don't have breasts.'

The doctor finds this amusing. 'Women always think that, but they only know their own breasts. I've seen a lot more over the years.'

True, but you'll never know what it feels like to be continually confronted with their existence, will you? Cover them, protect them or bare them some more? When mine first appeared, I spent the first year forgetting I had them, until a boy in my class intervened, saying I was no longer Fanny Flat-chest and really should start wearing a bra.

'They don't really feel like they're part of me . . . ' On the recording you hear my voice get higher; I almost understand what I mean and I'm angling for assistance. Silence from the doctor, after all his previous smooth talk. Finally he says that, in his experience, women who don't get implants have a harder time psychologically after the operation. He shrugs off all my questions about risks, leakage, waking up at night and no longer knowing what cold weight is hanging from your chest—negligible risks that barely ever happen.

Stay with it, Antiboy, focus and ask straightforward questions. But the conversation is full of invisible young women frolicking between us in their bikinis. By now we are discussing breasts like hairstyles; not every hairstyle suits everyone. So I ask to see photos of operations he has performed. He clicks open a slideshow showing a pared breast, a red flap of skin hanging down over the ribs and the fatty tissue visible. He quickly puts his hand over half the screen and clicks further, past bruises and contusions. A whole series of pictures flash past before he is able to show me a pair of breasts that look like tennis balls under a sheet. I look at them and try to want them, to want them like those other women do. I've come here with a high risk factor for cancer and the doctor's idea of consolation is to keep on telling me I won't be ugly afterwards.

If only I could interrupt him and say, 'Put on all your clothes at once. Pants and vest, shirt, tie, belt and trousers, long socks, jacket, big winter coat, or better still, a down-filled ski jacket, a scarf and a fur hat and jump in the water. Once everything is soaked through and pulls you down, once you've been treading water until you can barely keep going, then you'll know how heavy my body is. I can tell you love your white coat, even if there's a little coffee stain on the collar. You love to walk these corridors surrounded by junior doctors. If I were to make you walk down the corridor in a scruffy tracksuit, or skinny jeans, or—and neither of us can imagine this—a flowery dress, if you had to operate in a flowery dress, wouldn't you explain to each patient, "This isn't who I am?"'

But given he is going to add his signature in the form of scars on my chest, I don't say anything and just fix my eyes on the coffee stain on his collar. Until he explains that if I really insist on being flat, it will be such a simple operation that he won't be the one performing it. He's overqualified. I'll have to make a new appointment with another plastic surgeon and explain all over again that I don't want implants that I can't take off when I go to bed.

MY DAD TELLS ME that he and Mum almost broke up at the start. Since he was brought up to be a pacifist, he wanted to do community rather than military service. He could do this in the Netherlands or in the tropics. His father had been a doctor of tropical medicine in Indonesia, his mother a head nurse. That's how he pictured himself and Mum, the two of them running a hospital there, but she didn't want to go. She said, 'There's nothing for me in the tropics.'

He thought about it for a week and then swapped his dream for a person. She was standing at the stove, stirring a pan, when he came to tell her he was staying in the Netherlands for her. She barely responded.

Fifteen years later she said her love for him had dried up. Toni was three, I was an eighteen-month-old baby. And again he decided to stay—he wanted a family. He knew that she'd fight for the children should they divorce, because they fought about everything, so he said, 'Do whatever you need to get by, but we're staying married.'

We're having lunch in a restaurant when he tells me this. My father doesn't cook food, he orders it, so we often meet in restaurants. He says stuff like 'You kids didn't exactly grow up in a warm family,' in a brisk tone of voice.

'Did you ever think Mum might be lesbian?' I asked. An anonymous person sent a rose with rainbow petals to Mum's funeral. And when people came up to give their condolences, one woman took my hand, leaned in and said, 'Give me a call if you ever want to know who your mother really was.'

Dad studies a vegan fried egg made from half a peach, then spears it with his fork so it doesn't slide away when he cuts it.

'No, not really. Everyone's on a spectrum in terms of sexuality, right? Me too.'

'Mum as well?'

'When she was at uni, there were these two women. One of them liked to wear a brown velvet suit. They were both very interested in your mother and she in them so I encouraged her to experiment. But your mum was all talk, when it actually came down to it, she was too much of a coward. I'm more adventurous.'

'So nothing happened?'

'I even suggested joining in.'

I clap a hand over my eyes but still see him grinning. 'Dad, there was someone at the funeral who said I didn't really know Mum, that I should call her if I wanted to know more.'

He calmly pricks some rocket onto his forkful of peach. 'That must have been Clarice. She's always stirring things up.'

'Who was . . . ?'

'I can give you her number, if you want. You can have a chat with her.'

He sends me a screenshot of her number and asks whether this has anything to do with me only wearing men's clothes these days. I've had my head shaved too. A woman sitting next to me in the hairdresser's sighed that if she did that, her husband would kick her out. They gave me my ponytail to take home in a brown-paper bag.

'I feel more attractive dressed like this.'

I don't tell him that I asked Mort to marry me. I'd measured his ring finger with a piece of string when he was asleep, but then I asked him before I could get a ring made, with just that string in my pocket. Mort said, 'No, thank you. I don't want to be Freddy Mercury's girlfriend.'

And I tried to explain to Mort that I was attracted to women, but also to him, that it really didn't matter to me, but he said it should matter to me, just like it mattered to him that I no longer felt like a woman. Now that he knew, he found it impossible to touch me.

'Wouldn't you have rather married some-one who was happier to be with you?' I ask Dad.

Dad gives me a sullen look over his peach. 'All of her friends say I was her rock, that I really helped her a lot.'

I take hold of his hand with the loose skin around the knuckles. 'Of course you did, Dad.'

I sit on the warm part of the sofa, the bit by the window that catches the sunlight and look at the screenshot of Clarice's number. If Mum had had an affair it would explain a lot—the daily arguments with Dad, the way she seemed to walk in and out of our family. Dad always defended her, saying she couldn't help it, love-lessness was in her genes and she'd been abandoned as a child herself. My mother wasn't very curious about her roots. She never went back to Aruba, where she was born, the island she left when she was five. When her estranged father telephoned her and she heard his voice for the first time in two decades, she hung up without speaking. I've always thought you should listen carefully to what's happening inside you, that's how your life becomes real. But maybe that's not true either, maybe that longing for life is your life.

I click away the screenshot and open YouTube as a distraction. Tiffany Pollard is a

New York celebrity who on *UK Celebrity Big Brother* has to share the house with a number of Brits, including the favourite, Gemma. Gemma gave Tiffany a pair of high heels because she had to spend her birthday in the house, far from friends and family, but then she snatched back the heels an episode later when Tiffany insulted her. Tiffany is asked on camera for her reaction to the shoe drama.

'I will let Gemma know that she is a fat cunt and the shoes that she gave me were not something I would particularly buy myself. They were old-maiden type of shoes. And she said the shoes were meant to be worn on a beautiful woman. So if that's the case, she should have put them back on the rack, and she shouldn't have even purchased them, because she was unqualified to own those shoes if that's the case. And um, I think Gemma's just a disgrace. She's a disgrace to women who are actually beautiful and classy and she doesn't even have the vernacular she thinks she possesses. Someone lied to her several times and told her that she was fly, hot and sexy and beautiful, and she's nothing like that, she's nothing of the sort.'

But who, who lied to Gemma that she's a beautiful woman? Who lied to me? I often asked my mother if she thought she was beautiful; for years her answer was no. Until she was on her deathbed and she said, 'I didn't know I was beautiful.'

'WHAT SHOULD I CALL YOU when we're talking about the past?' I asked Slimane a couple of weeks after we'd met for coffee.

'Use my new name,' he said. His mother had come up with his new name. But how was I supposed to think about him in the past tense?

'You thought at the time that I was a girl, and it's all right to remember that,' he said, and I didn't know whether this was a reproach or permission. It had been important to me as a nineteen-year-old that I'd seen him as a woman, because this was the first girl I took home to meet my parents.

Just before my sister moved out for good, she summoned us all to the living room to meet her boyfriend, a fifty-three-year-old taxi driver she'd met at a backgammon tournament. She was nineteen at the time. My father was fifty-one and behaved like a perfect host. He kept asking if anyone wanted more tea and he'd arranged sticky cubes of Turkish delight on a plate. Mum sat at the window reading a women's magazine. She lowered it now and again to cast a questioning glance at the couple. I'd been fetched from my bed for this introduction, the night before I'd been up late drinking beer at the cinema. My temples pounding, I looked at my sister perched on the taxi driver's lap, even though we had enough chairs. The man was wearing a leather waist-coat and a faded grey shirt. He had to admit, he said, that he had a daughter older than my sister. My father asked after the rest of the family's health. I snorted with laughter but no one else joined in. This was my cue to jump to my feet and head to the kitchen for some breakfast. As I warmed up a steamed bun in the microwave, I reflected on Toni's motives. Before I knew it, her taxi driver was standing behind me with barely a hand's width between us for me to turn around in. I held my stale hungover breath.

'Are you by any chance an Aquarius?' he asked.

'No.'

'Libra?' He folded his bare arms, his leather waistcoat creaking.

'No.'

'What then?'

'Scorpio.'

He gave me a contented nod. 'Ah, that explains it. I never get on with Scorpios.'

Raised voices in the living room, my sister talking to my dad, Mum's nervous laughter drowning everything else out.

The first time I took Slimane home with me, I'd been living on my own for a year but I still thought of my childhood bedroom as 'home'. We weren't in a relationship but he still left chocolate bars for me under the carrier straps of my bike rack. To do this, he had to walk along the long row of bikes parked at the station until he found mine. One day, an ex-boyfriend of mine who wanted to get back together had left me a postcard that said, 'You're the wonderfulest.' Slimane had crossed out my ex's name and added his own.

My dad sat in the same chair as when the taxi driver had come round. He brought out the Turkish delight for Slimane too. Mum was clattering around in the kitchen.

'Excuse me,' I said, getting up.

Mum was kneeling in front of a kitchen cupboard, which still contained cans from the 1980s, long before I was born. As long as the can wasn't bulging, the contents were still fairly edible, she claimed.

'We're waiting for you.'

'I'm busy,' she said.

Slimane and my dad were exchanging pleasantries in the living room. When I sat down next to Slimane on the sofa, he patted my knee. Now my father made his excuses and went to fetch my mother from the kitchen. He planted her on a chair in front of the window and went to make a pot of tea. Mum sat with her arms crossed, her gaze averted. Slimane put an arm around me. Mum looked at every-thing in the room except at that arm. She's afraid, I thought, much to my surprise. I began to wriggle out of Slimane's embrace but he pulled me closer.

'Shall we take our bags upstairs?' I suggested.

'Good plan, darling,' Slimane said and my mother frowned.

There was a king-sized water bed in my bedroom. He jumped on it immediately and pulled me down with him. We lay on top of the duvet, undulating.

'As a kid I always used to fantasize that I was in a canoe covered with flowers, floating down the river before I went to sleep. It had something to do with dying,' I said. 'I was born in this bed. The water has been changed since then, though.'

Slimane got under the duvet and held it open invitingly but I shook my head. I didn't know whether he'd come out to his family, only that his parents had fled their country because of a war. One time he told me about a professor who'd had to leave behind his collection of books but in the Netherlands he'd found some cardboard boxes dumped on the street containing the very books he was missing. He didn't want to tell me whether it was someone he knew, but the point to remember was that everything came back to you in the end.

He lay quietly next to me without wandering hands. His head was on my shoulder, then on my chest. In the afternoon light, lines ran through his hair, glowing threads. I wished he could read minds. I wished I could share the colours with him. I wished that the first girl I'd introduced to my parents was in love with me. The door flew open. Instinctively he withdrew his head, hiding like a tortoise. My mother stood in the doorway with her hands on her hips.

'So now you have a beard?!' she cried.

Slimane's hair was covering my face. He began to shake with laughter under the duvet.

'No, Mum,' I said, brushing Slimane's curls from my chin. Mum looked like she wanted to say something. She looked so helpless. Slimane's fit of giggles, muffled by the duvet, was much too loud to be genuine.

'Don't you dare tell Grandma,' Mum said, closing the door again.

As long as he stayed there, I could pretend I was laughing too. I worked my lips into a tight grimace. But when Slimane surfaced, panting, and rolled on top of me, I said, at close proximity to his face, 'We mustn't laugh at my mum.'

OUTSIDE ON THE STREETS, a 'trans summer of rage' is underway. There are demonstrations in Dam Square with protesters demanding faster, better treatment and commemorating friends who died before reaching the top of the waiting list. The newspaper coverage is extensive, so, in the absence of a referral to the gender-reassignment clinic (there's a two- to three-year waiting list), I start reading. Research, interviews and novels, everything I can get my hands on that features trans people and cross-dressers and genderqueers and non-binary characters. I read about liberation and euphoria, about love and anal sex as a spiritual experience. Every columnist has a different opinion, they question whether the phenomenon actually exists and whether we aren't taking things too far. The people passing judgement aren't just professors of gender studies or social workers. Historians, philosophers and writers are suddenly experts, imagining themselves capable of performing open-heart surgery because they too have hearts. They keep trying to define what a man is, and what a woman, but actually they're trying to determine what a human is. I wait for a sign, for permission. A friend says, 'If you don't decide, time will decide for you.'

I ask women *when* they feel like a woman and they respond:

When someone bothers me on the train.

I once got boxed in by a man in a van when I was walking down the street but I ran away quick, he couldn't unlock his door in time.

Men are always touching you up on the dance floor, it's part of life.

When I brush my hair.

In a leopard-print bikini.

When my insides hurt.

For me it's really all to do with my breasts.

In my friendships with other women, the way we take care of each other.

I don't actually know why I call myself a woman, but I know I am one.

When it's dark and I walk with my house keys between my knuckles.

Someone calling me a whore when I cross the street.

At the hairdressers, reading a magazine with my hair packed in silver foil and an itchy scalp. Or when a strand of hair gets stuck to my lip gloss.

During sex.

When he left me and I stood in the doorway screaming like a goddess of retribution that I'd never been happy, never, that he should think that I'd ever, for a second, enjoyed being with him, not in all those years, that he had a small dick and was shit in bed and that I'd sucked off his friends, and knowing I'd have to apologize later but not then, then I wanted to hurt him, and cause all kinds of damage that some other woman would have to repair, I still remember which dress I was wearing as I screamed at him. Whenever I see it in my wardrobe, I think: revenge dress.

In the summer.

Construction workers.

I've never thought about it and I don't think I need to. If I wasn't one, I'd know, wouldn't I? Can I ask *you* a question? Have you ever felt like you were betraying woman-kind?

If gender is a construct, how can you say you're not a woman?

In the women's department, in the ladies toilets, in the changing room.

In the sea.

To be honest, I'm not sure. No one paid any attention to this kind of thing when we were growing up. So it feels a bit . . . too late for this question? And I don't say that with any regret.

The man I ask when he feels like a man says that men have the highest chance of being murdered by another man and that men can be sexually assaulted by men too and that women always forget this, they're so quick to claim the role of victim. One friend says, 'The label *man* doesn't mean much to me: *friend*, *brother* or *son* are more meaningful to me,' and another man sighs that it's part of him, just like his feet.

'Have you always known?' people ask me in turn, but who is going to love me? I don't want long hair any more (*but who is going to love you?*), if only I had a flat chest (*but what if you take off your clothes and the other person expects to see breasts?*), I don't know which girl you're talking to (*just enjoy the attention*), and I've never been who I should be, I've always been in-between (*which doesn't exist*), there was always the hope that one day I'd get the hang of being a girl, that I'd finally turn into the right one. Yes, I always knew but I called it emptiness. Something was missing that other people did have. I only knew that love was something you dreamed of, and all the while something was screaming under my skin (*escape*) and I spent so long staring at my feet to figure out my gender.

IT'S A MONTH SINCE the operation and the white beeping is now only audible in the background. Being able to walk outside in the fresh air again makes me feel almost drunk. The sun-kissed trees, people sauntering along. And Mort and I are walking among them, hand in hand. It's the best thing in the world, walking hand in hand with Mort, and not only because I still trip over the uneven cobblestones at times. I can feel a heartbeat between our palms. At his side I feel like a beauty with my flat chest, my jacket open. Under my T-shirt I'm wearing the compression vest which protects the wounds and stops the empty pockets of skin from filling with fluid. Mort zips the vest open and shut each day. He's fetched medicine for me, sat me on a folding chair and showered me, and done all the shopping. Everyone who comes over says how lovingly he's taking care of me and then I look at his happy face and am convinced that we belong together. But once the visitors leave, he says how exhausted he is and that he's moving out as soon as I'm better.

'We're going to stay together, right?' I ask again. He swings my arm back and forward in response. The scars under my armpits tighten. Green heart-shaped leaves grow on the slope that dogs race down. A family is having a picnic with a disposable BBQ, its flames are shooting up high. They let the meat scorch, laugh and drink as their toddler waddles off in a saggy nappy. Six months ago, Mort and I had stickers made with our faces on them and stuck them on meter cupboards and lampposts. Everywhere we go, we see ourselves. On the stickers I still have long hair and breasts. It reminds me of that long night in hospital but I'm through the worst of it, the worst part was falling on my way to the toilet and not being able to get back up again. After that night, Mort sneaked in before visiting hours, lifted me into a red wheelchair and took me home.

And now I'm walking around in another pair of shoes that pinch, I accidentally bought the wrong size. My squashed toes drown out the pain in my chest, my cheeks slowly burn and there are so many routes we can take, weaving past the other people or over the grass. Now I no longer have breast cancer to fear, I only need to watch out when crossing the road.

I lean towards Mort for a kiss. Our second kiss, years ago, was outside a bar. We'd already kissed inside it, but out in the night air we didn't know how to act, so he offered me a cigarette. As I took a drag, he threw himself into my arms and accidentally knocked me over. My head hit the cobbles. Drunk, dazed and with Mort on top of me, covered by his coat, I disappeared into our embrace, until the forgotten cigarette started burning through my polyester dress. Around the burn hole, the fabric melted onto my breast. Later it became a scar and even something to laugh about, each kiss an echo of that fall.

But Mort pushes my face away. 'Not here. Can't you see those men?'

'Which men?'

'Don't look now but that man there. He thinks we're both guys.'

'So what?'

He lets go of my hand and steps to the side so that someone else can fit in the space between us. Just two friends out for a walk.

'Are we never going to kiss in public again?' I ask.

He turns around abruptly and heads back to the flat. I look at the couples lying on the grassy knoll. Last summer, I lay on that slope reading a book about a mistress who is always waiting for her married lover to call. There was a passage in which she's allowed to visit his apartment for the first time because his wife is on holiday. On her way to the toilet, she passes an open wardrobe in their bedroom and can't resist slipping her feet into his wife's high heels, and then comes the droning realization that the other woman really does exist. It's not the same, I'm not a mistress, not a secret, just someone he no longer wants to walk down the street with. His pride has turned into shame. I try to imagine what it would be like, putting on a dress, styling my hair in a feminine way, so that he'd want to show me off again and wouldn't have to wonder what others saw when they looked at us. I would disappear back into myself. I run after Mort in my painfully pinching shoes. He has stopped at a traffic light which still has two stickers of our smiling faces on it, peeling at the edges.

'Shall we get some new stickers made?' I ask.

His shoulders slump and this reminds me of the sulky pictures of him as a toddler. In one of them, he's sucking his thumb while holding a ball of socks wrapped in a tea towel in his other hand. It was his comfort object and he took it everywhere with him. I said as a joke that I was his new comfort object and that his mum was paying me to hold his hand. And that I didn't actually exist, that I was a ball of socks in a tea towel that he thought was a girl. He replied that I was quite comprehensive for a psychotic delusion.

'It doesn't matter what those men see because I'm not a boy,' I say. 'Would it help if I grew my hair again?'

Mort sighs. 'I don't want to hold you back.'

'You're not holding me back. I only want to hear you say that I'm still attractive. That I haven't changed.'

'But you have changed.'

'I was always like this. Everything you did, you did with me.'

During the operation, they removed quite a lot of skin from my chest but not the part with our scar on it. The cigarette burn, permission to be ravaged.

Mort doesn't reply.

'I'm happy,' I say, to gauge whether I'm lying.

AFTER THE VISIT TO MY PARENTS', Slimane and I stopped messaging each other so often. Despite my despair, I kept my texts light and cheery and in the end this seemed to work— we arranged to meet up in a snack bar late one night. He watched me eat a sloppy pork sandwich with peanut sauce and shook his head. Then he dipped a soggy chip in the ketchup and stirred it around. In the big glass windows you could see the darkness outside but also our yellow reflection. Slimane said, as though it was a matter of no importance, that he was dating a man now too, with the ridiculous name of Wim. Had we slipped from being lovers back into being friends?

'So he's like forty?' I said.

'We have some great conversations.'

'But we do too, right?' I laid my hand on top of his and he didn't flick it away.

A group of drunk students stumbled in and Damian was among them. Since he broke up with his girlfriend, I ended up in his bed sometimes. After the sex, he'd whisper that I really mustn't fall in love with him, and he'd play guitar for me in his boxer shorts. I'd stopped sleeping with him because of Slimane. His friends went to order and he came over to our table.

'Hello ladies, enjoying yourselves?' He stayed on Slimane's side of the table.

'Sweetie,' Slimane asked me, 'have you had enough to eat?'

He fed me a cold chip as Damian looked on. Damian grinned and swayed back to his friends. Slimane and I leaned in towards each other, suddenly behaving like a couple. With every word we whispered, I became more of a stranger to myself.

'Who's he?' he hissed.

'My Wim.'

Paradiso nightclub was closing for the night and the clubbers poured onto the street.

The snack bar's owner, a tall man with a moustache, locked the door. The first inebriated partygoer reached the door and pushed at it. The owner stood behind the glass, arms folded and shook his head. We were in a strip-lit aquarium which was attracting more and more tired and hungry people. They pressed their palms to the window right next to my face. Raised hands, fingers spread, pounding the glass to the slow beat of my heart. My sexual orientation was being wanted. I was sick to death of feeling unwanted. The owner let us out, one by one, opening the door a crack and shouting *no* repeatedly at the newly sobered-up zombies who pleaded for just one hamburger, a portion of chips, please!?

Damian hung back so that I had to squeeze past him. He whispered, 'See you later maybe?'

'Bye,' I said and he grinned that Cheshire Cat grin again.

'What a scumbag,' Slimane said. We walked along the street without a plan. 'Like you're a dog and all he has to do is whistle.'

'He's better than nothing,' I said, but he didn't respond to this. We paused next to a red bike with a carrier rack. 'This one's his.'

Slimane squatted down next to the back wheel. 'Do I need to slay a dragon for you?' His fingers picked at the air valve. 'What do you talk about with a dude like him?' he asked.

'A few seconds after having sex, I asked him what he was thinking about and he said *the Tour de France.*'

'Oh honey, that's tragic.'

'It's not tragic, it's honest.' I kicked his spokes and kept to myself the fact that I'd been in love with Damian for a while. Right at the start, we'd laughed a lot and shared earbuds to listen to songs together. But imperceptibly, things turned darker. When I went round, Damian would tell me I couldn't sleep over practically before I was over the threshold, and I had to do breathing exercises on his loo to relax my body.

Slimane pulled out the air valve. We watched as the tyre sank to the pavement. At the end of the dug-up street, roadworkers were standing up to their chests in a hole. Sparks flew from the sewage pipe that they were cutting in half with their circular saw. Slimane asked me above the racket what I saw in a person like that.

'You're making this bigger than it is,' I said.

He smiled sadly. 'Does he understand you the way you want to be understood?'

'It's nice to be desired.'

Slimane said he'd call and left me standing there.

In the days, months that followed, whenever I called his number, the phone rang out, and I filled his inbox with messages. Maybe he didn't want to disappear because of me, but in spite of me. He wanted to figure out how to become himself without becoming a dragon.

In the end, the only thing I was sure of was that there had been sparks, hands that had banged harder and harder against a window. I kept a note that Slimane had slipped into my pocket three weeks before the snack-bar incident. It said, 'You have to stop comparing yourself to other people. I only compare myself to God.'

On my way back to the snack bar where I'd parked my bike, I sauntered so slowly that I almost tripped over a paving stone. My phone kept vibrating in my pocket, Damian had already sent me three text messages.

'Are you two having a pyjama party? Can I join in? Hey?'

Damian's favourite songs tended to feature ill-fated girls with messy eyeliner. Of course they wore summer dresses, drove motorbikes and drunkenly set off fireworks. They danced with their eyes closed and went to bed with all and sundry. I think Damian thought he was paying me a compliment when he compared me to them. Did those girls actually exist or did everyone start behaving like that because of the constant background chorus of sexy decline, of women you could laugh at because they were once the prettiest girl in the class but now, in middle age, they wore beige support tights, divas who got cancer and lost their hair, young superstars with smeared make-up on police headshots. Everyone was waiting for the overdose, the body found in the hotel room. They were variations on a theme: she was once so beautiful and now she's dead. Fathers and seedy lovers were added to the mix as plot details, somebody had destroyed or abandoned her. A man who closed the door behind him because he could no longer cope, leaving her crying on the bed. She screamed after him, grotesque in her despair, her dress slipping from her shoulder, her eyes two black holes.

I felt guilty towards all those women when I rang Damian's doorbell. But, I imagined telling them, as I climbed the stairs, that didn't they know better than anyone how easy it was to disappear? You had to find someone who carried on when you said stop, who only saw a vague outline of you beyond a certain point, who apologized for your pain with the excuse that he was drunk. That was how you let yourself down.

There was a McDonald's down the road from his place which was open until 4 a.m. I sat there at the window on the streetside and chomped on a cheeseburger. If he walked past, he'd see me, but I knew he'd fallen asleep after the sex. I'd wiped myself on his duvet cover and again in the loo with toilet paper because I saw a trace of blood. After that I'd let myself out. Having sex with him was disappearing under a layer of dark ice, a place where nobody could find me, where I wasn't even present myself.

I queued up for a 'Chicken 6' with sweet-and-sour sauce. The boy behind the counter spun his cap a quarter of a turn and moved up a cash register. He gestured to a girl with green eyeshadow and platinum curls standing behind me in the queue.

'I only help pretty girls,' he said with a grin. The girl rolled her eyes before stepping out of the queue and ordering from him. Numb, I gripped my tray which already had a cheeseburger wrapper on it. Wasn't I pretty? That explained a lot. The chicken nuggets were luke-warm when they arrived in their carton, and specked with salt. My left leg wouldn't stop shaking; I rested a hand on it once I'd sat back down at a table. The placemat had facts about McDonald's on it. Did I know that the first McDonald's in the Netherlands opened in 1971? Yes, I knew that. I'd given a talk about McDonald's at school when I was eleven or twelve. I'd told my classmates they served snake nuggets in Thailand and pea soup in the 1970s in the Netherlands. I'd saved the paper place-mats covered in grease marks and hung them on the wall above my bed. Not posters of boy-bands but dancing French fries and, strangely enough, I'd also pinned up a threatening letter I'd received that first year of secondary school. It was a white sheet of A4 with cut-out news-paper letters that spelled 'We know what you did. Confess!' The capital W came from a dis-count store's advertising brochure. I had no idea what I was supposed to confess to or who had sent the letter.

I used a chewed ballpoint to scrawl 'Yeah, cos you're so fucking gorgeous?' on a paper napkin. I laid it on the counter but the boy with his cap askew didn't even look at it as he scrunched it up and tossed it in the bin.

The road outside should have been straight but seemed to be winding. Walking with my bike, I followed the tram tracks, crossing them at right angles, into the street with the night-club Jimmy Woo, passed an Indian restaurant, and suddenly I was standing in front of Damian's front door again. Bent deep over the handlebars, I turned around and the back wheel jammed, almost pulling me over as I walked. The faceless shop dummies in the H&M window were positioned like they were having a conversation. *How are you doing? Wonderful, wonderful!* Their hands were raised, which went with their carefree lives, bared shoulders and floral tops. I turned back into the side street, but now the back-pedal brake jammed, so forward then instead. Please stop shaking. If I stopped and stood still, maybe the street would start moving and carry me home. The problem with being erased was that it was so hard to come back. When you saw the devastation, you dived back under the ice, stared into the streetlights until you saw black glass. My broken heart pounded in my crotch.

What a funny place to rupture.

I DIDN'T WANT TO BE a girl or a boy, I wanted to be a child again. That was why I went back to drawing stick figures with hands like rakes. Not long after I fell into the ditch at school, we were split up: separate changing rooms for boys and girls after gym, different reading levels, small groups around a table you could choose yourself. Teachers no longer determined whom you sat next to. On her first day, Toni had become best friends with a girl everyone thought was our sister. She even posed with us for the school photos. But the children I asked to be my family ran away giggling. I walked to the football section of the playground, in slow motion so that it took longer. Once I got there, the boys I called out to ignored me. I walked even more slowly to the bike sheds where some girls were sitting on the ground chatting. When people are talking it's

89

hard to join in, you can only eavesdrop at a distance and hope someone asks you something. What did you have to do to be a child? When I was eight my teacher had called my parents regularly, expressing her concerns, something I only discovered years later when my mother's diaries were left in the loo as reading material.

To help me, the teacher picked me first to give a book talk to the class. It had to be about a children's book. I would have preferred to read out an article I'd found in a women's magazine in which a mother admitted loving one of her children more than the other. I thought about that article before falling asleep at night. I was the favourite child, surely? Toni had broken a bone in her foot once but I was still whole. In the end I chose *Regrets* by Carry Slee. It was about a boy who committed suicide after being bullied at school. I thought it was the perfect book to set the tone so that my classmates didn't come up with childish books about football prodigies or pony clubs.

I was allowed to sit beside the teacher and the rest of the children sat in a circle. The only difference from a Dutch birthday party was I didn't have sweets to hand out. *Regrets* is about a boy David who is popular and Jochem who is bullied. After the gym lesson, the bullies want to put a bra on Jochem who always laughs along and tries to avoid being bullied, but what he actually needs is a friend. When nobody helps him, he drowns himself in a lake. I looked at the other children as I talked, at their blond quiffs and pink ears and horrified expressions. As an eight-year-old, I didn't usually talk for this long. The teacher took the book from me and looked at the cover.

'This is a 13+ book,' she told the class.

'Is it based on a true story, Miss?' Robin asked.

'David promised to stand up for Jochem but because he was in love with a girl, he forgot and then it was too late . . . ' I droned on, because my book talk was a kind of prayer. They had to stop using my gym bag as a football and laughing at me, or saying that there was no room for me at their table. I was already trying my hardest to have the right thoughts, so now it was up to them, someone had to sacrifice themselves and be my only friend. But the teacher cut my talk short and told Robin that it was only a book. She let us out early for break but held me back for a moment. Squatting down next to my chair, she searched for the right tone.

'Suicide isn't a good topic for a book talk,' she said in the end.

'Didn't the other children know about it yet?'

The teacher gave me a kind look and replied, 'No, it was still a secret.'

It was also still a secret that you could be proud of yourself—that you could stick a Post-it next to your mirror that said *I'm better than normal, I'm abnormal*—that once you were an adult, you could buy yourself a suit and a shirt that fits your flat chest like a glove. How your body tingled when the shop assistant did up your tie. You could join a march and be surrounded by rainbow flags. Strangers would call you brave until you stood there unable to utter a word.

And when you've been having a hard time for days, remember: the secret is that you've been dropped on a mysterious bare planet, but you have to keep on transmitting signals. How else will your people find you and come to get you? One of those people is going to cover your flat chest in kisses and ask, 'Does this hurt?' And you're going to lie: 'Of course not,' so that it never stops.

BECAUSE IT'S A WOODLAND CEMETERY and there aren't any gravestones, I often have trouble finding my mum. In the summer, in particular, when the purple thistles are waist high, the graves are invisible. The people lying here in their coffins made of untreated wood picked a place on the edge of the trees or in the open meadow. They can rest in peace, surrounded by oaks and beeches with a flat section of tree trunk at the head of their graves. My hands tucked in my sleeves, I pull apart the prickly bushes and stamp the weeds flat as I walk over the dead.

Charlotte has brought cake and fried chicken so we can have a picnic at my mum's feet. I sprinkle tea from a thermos flask over her grave and take out a plastic container of raspberries. The last time she came, my cousin left a hand-painted pebble on the tree-trunk

94

plaquette; the colours have run. Mushrooms have spread across a piece of wet paper, a now illegible note.

'Would you leave us alone for a moment?'

Charlotte picks up the thermos and the Tupperware tubs and goes to sit a few metres away, cross-legged, out of earshot. I absent-mindedly roll a raspberry between my finger-tips. Mum's last wish was for Queen's 'I Want to Break Free' to be played as the coffin was lowered into the grave. My brother-in-law stood next to the hole in his tailored grey suit holding computer speakers and an iPad and pressed *play* during a silence punctuated with sobs. The coffin started to move when the opening guitar chords were sounded. It rolled down to the bottom, supported by ropes and pulleys. A gust of wind blew the trees in our direction as though they were trying to hear us.

But life just wouldn't go on. We wouldn't get used to living life without her, no matter how hard we tried.

Somebody squealed with grief, it was me. Mort held onto my wrist but I wasn't planning on throwing myself into the hole, I'd never steal my mother's thunder like that. Her funeral had been arranged like a show, with a choir and dance moves and a pre-recorded message in which she let out a truly blood-curdling scream to give everyone in the church a fright. She wanted to leave her mark, something people would talk about, she'd waited until the very end to draw so much attention to herself.

In hushed tones so that Charlotte can't hear, I ask Mum what it was like to wake up without a breast. She never let me see her crumpled scar, the bathroom door would slam shut behind her. Why did we never talk about dying? In the week before she died, when she could still lie in her own bed if she climbed the stairs very slowly, I asked her what I should do. I asked whether she missed her breast and when I should have my ovaries removed. Should I try to have children first or wasn't it worth the risk? The bedspread she lay under was almost too heavy already.

'You should stay with Mort,' Mum said at last.

Not an answer but an order.

'Can you imagine,' she panted, 'people being depressed and lying in bed for days?'

Mum tiredly tilted her head to her shoulder. She cut the thread that had been strung between us the year when I had been unable to eat or sleep. The year in which my friends gave up on me one by one, my dad kept complaining that he couldn't sleep for worrying and walked around stony-faced as though I were already dead, my sister said I was acting like a teenager, doing anything to get attention. She offered to help by selling my shoes. That year Mum brought round groceries each week. The aubergines from her previous visit would lie rotting in the vegetable drawer. She piled bottles of beetroot juice on top of other unopened bottles, and threw a pair of jeans at me. One of its sharp buttons left a scratch next to my eye. Get dressed, put up your hair, you've got nothing to cry about. She impatiently pushed me downstairs. I held onto the banister with both hands because my head was spinning, the escalators I hallucinated on the ceiling glided down with us. It was freezing cold that summer, I shivered in a woolly jumper and she took my arm and steered me past the dark gleam of the canal. She kept on repeating that committing suicide was the worst thing a child could do to its parents. I clawed my way through the days on a mixture of guilt and watery microwave porridge. Sometimes I didn't even open the door to her when she came round, or I texted her half an hour before to cancel. It had nothing to do with her, me not fitting in, I was constantly searching for a way out. Nevertheless, she carried on dragging me out of bed and ignoring the text messages begging her not to come. Just before she died, Mum forgot all that she'd done for me.

Pink raspberry mush drips down my thumb, I'd squeezed too hard by accident.

Last week I finally called Clarice. I said I was missing my mum and wanted to talk about her. She said she could make time immediately.

She'd got to know my mum right after she'd had breast cancer, when she felt so empty and lonely. They'd gone to a spiritual group's meetings together. Clarice started to explain the teachings of the Ridhwan school to me, but I interrupted her.

'Why did you say at my mother's funeral that I didn't really know her?'

Silence. 'Did I say that?'

'Yes.'

'I don't know what I meant by that,' Clarice said.

'I hoped you were going to say that my mum was lesbian,' I said.

'You know, people always thought we were a couple. We sometimes went away together and she came round after work every other Friday. She'd lie on the sofa while I cooked. She had her own red blanket she'd cover herself with. But your mum kept the weekends free for your dad, she was strict about that.'

'And you never thought . . . ?'

'Your mum was restless, dissatisfied. But she didn't want to know what was at the root of it.'

All I could say for certain was she'd had me, hadn't she? Whatever her sexual preferences, she'd had children. Toni and I exist because she stayed with my dad, despite it all.

Charlotte wraps her arms around me. I hadn't heard her approaching.

'Do you know what Mort said when you'd had the operation and were still coming round from the anaesthetic?' she asked. 'When we were walking around in circles outside the hospital? He said he always wanted to stay with you, whoever you are, no matter what.'

'Well, he never says that to me. He says it in interviews, on camera, and to the talk show host, Humberto Tan, but never when we're alone. Why does he never say it when we're alone?' I ask, wiping my eyes.

I throw the squashed raspberry onto the grave. Go on, grow into a bush that will cover Mum forever, a bush with prickles and round, shiny fruit for the birds. Charlotte hands me some more coconut cake. We carry on picnicking and now and then she says something to Mum, including her in our conversation. I'm so grateful to Charlotte, my mum only met her a few times but she was so fond of her. Maybe Charlotte would kick the door in if things fell apart, she'd undoubtedly help me more gently out of my bed than Mum did. But I would never ask her. My mum is the only person I'd ever ask to do that.

I don't ever want to fall between the cracks again.

'Charlotte,' I say, 'I need to tell you something,' and I try to describe everything at once, my fear of death, my doubts, being in-between and left out. At first I can't look at her, but we have to be brave. Her eyes shine like searchlights.

WHAT WILL I WEAR when I go swimming this summer? The scars are still fresh and have to be kept out of the sun, so maybe an old-fashioned striped men's swimming costume with sleeves. The water of the IJ sparkles behind Amsterdam's Central Station, it would be so easy to jump in. Pedestrians stream from the ferry, bicycles and mopeds crossing their path, a collision constantly a hairbreadth away. I am out of harm's way by the taxi rank where my dad is coming to pick me up. We are going to visit my grandparents at the nursing home. Dad has warned me that they won't know who I am any more, but I don't recognize myself either. He pulls up in his new red car, there's still space between the taxis and he gestures for me to hurry up, but I stand on the pavement a moment longer before squeezing into his stuffy car. When I get in at last he's itching to drive off as fast as possible because it's a no-parking zone.

'Hang on a minute, I need to tell you something.'

'Can you shut the door first?'

I shut the door but zip down the window. A taxi at the front of the line moves off. Dad's eyes nervously track the cars. We're surrounded by traffic and here, this is where I can say it, against this backdrop of coming and going.

'Dad, I've got a new name.'

My father stares straight ahead, his hands on the steering wheel of the idling car.

'Can you call me Antiboy from now on?'

'Is that a stage name?'

'No, but a female name no longer feels good. It makes me dizzy.'

'And Antiboy makes you feel good?' he asks.

'Yes.'

'I'll do my best,' Dad says. 'But now we really have to get going, or we'll be late for Grandma.'

On the motorway, he strings together one story after another and forgets to keep his hands on the wheel as he tells them. I don't say much and rest my head against the window. A couple of people are already getting used to my new name. Somebody said it was a choice made out of love for myself. A twinge of pain runs through my chest. The plastic surgeon said there wouldn't be any feeling left under my skin once all the nerve endings were removed, but my chest still tingles like a leg that's gone to sleep. The surgeon couldn't say how long this barbed-wire feeling would last, it was a signal my brain was struggling to understand and that's why it translated it as pain. I was told in order to recover, I should lovingly kiss and caress the affected body part, press on the pain until it became something new.

But should you press on pain? When I was visiting my dad recently, I found Mum's diary next to the loo. I was no longer looking for hidden secrets, I just wanted to see her hand-writing. In the middle of a list of what she'd eaten that day, she had written something about my father: 'Don't think, don't talk, don't feel when he's there.'

That was how they were able to stay together. And Mort and I had almost made it, too. But then Mort said that I was dead. We were standing beneath a streetlamp and he kept on repeating it, his face bathed in an orange glow. I tore open and that night in the hospital, the rot and the constant fear fell away from under my skin. I would never be able to speak to my mother again. I wanted to scream that *dead* was a swearword. He kept repeating it: a girl had died along the way. And still he'd carried on looking after me, until it almost broke him, couldn't I see? So I lied and said I was better, so that he could leave. He asked me to help him mourn the girl he had lost.

My grandma sits in her wheelchair in the spacious apartment. She grips my hand tightly as Grandad turns up the volume on his sports channel. Gymnasts are doing somersaults on a mat. Over the noise, I ask my half-deaf grandmother how she's doing. She looks at me searchingly.

'Who are you?'

I say my old name. She shakes her head and gives my dad a questioning look. He's sitting in the chair next to me. She's known him for longer, a son-in-law who visits regularly and writes down in a notebook which fruit he's brought. His own mother died young and he calls Grandma 'Ma'. On a low chest of drawers, there's a photo of my mum. It's the one they put on her coffin, taken just before she died. She frowns into the sunlight, which is typical of her, but I would have chosen a happier picture myself. My grandma is still holding my hand tightly, her lilac-varnished nails digging into my skin. But she addresses my dad, 'I can't see it. Who is this?'

'Whose child are you?' Grandad asks loudly.

'Your daughter's.'

Grandad shakes his head. 'She didn't have any children.'

On the wall there are framed photos of my cousins and school photos of my sister's kids. I wander through the apartment. On their bedroom wall, I come across a group picture of all of their grandchildren, taken when I was eleven. It's better than nothing. I take it off the hook and bring it to the living room.

'Look, that's me.'

My grandma takes the picture and holds it so loosely it almost slides off her lap. I take it back and hold it up to her face. She looks from the eleven-year-old girl in the photo to me, a rather overheated adult who towers above her and has a shaved head and a round face. The day that picture was taken, I was wearing skinny jeans for the first time. It was the summer before I started secondary school and I was hoping to find other people like me there. I put the frame down on the table and lower myself into the chair next to Grandma. She lays her veiny hand on mine again and gives it a squeeze and I wonder who I will be when I've forgotten everything in my old age. Which name will I answer to?

'I can see it's making you sad,' my dad says in strange, flat voice.

Grandma asks again who I am.

'Your grandchild.' I say my girl's name and then my new name, because my name is a word, I believe in words, that if I find the right word, everyone will come back.

Congratulations, people keep saying to me as if I've just been born.

———